KITTENS & CATS

BY
Michael Findlay

ILLUSTRATED BY
Jim Robins

MACDONALD

First published 1980

Macdonald Educational Ltd
Holywell House
Worship Street
London EC2A 2EN

© Macdonald Educational 1980
ISBN 0 356 06331 3 (paperback)
ISBN 0 356 06371 2 (hardback)

Printed by New Interlitho
Milan Italy

About this book

This book has been carefully planned to help you become an expert. Look for the special pages to find the information you need. **RECOGNITION** pages, with a **brown flash** in the top right-hand corner, contain all the essential information to know and remember. **PROJECT** pages, with a **grey border,** suggest some interesting ideas for things to do and make. At the end of the book there is a useful **REFERENCE** section.

Cats make good pets

A cat or kitten makes one of the most satisfactory pets. Providing you are not allergic to cats, they provide hours of happy enjoyment and are equally at home confined indoors or allowed full liberty. They are lithe and graceful, and are easy and inexpensive to care for.

Kittens and cats are available from a variety of sources - pet shops, breeders, animal welfare charities, and home-bred litters. These home-bred litters often produce the best cared-for kittens. Pedigree cats should always be purchased from a well known breeder and obviously cost considerably more than a 'mongrel' kitten.

Time for your kitten
Before owning a kitten, however, be sure you can devote plenty of time to giving it play periods, company and affection. Also think about costs of feeding, equipment, holiday boarding and vet's fees.

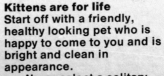

Kittens are for life
Start off with a friendly, healthy looking pet who is happy to come to you and is bright and clean in appearance.

Never select a solitary kitten of unknown origin unless you can be sure that it appears fit. If in doubt, ask your vet to check it as soon as possible.

Are its ears, eyes, nose and rear-end clean and its coat free from fleas? Are its litter mates also clear of these possible problems?

The hidden costs

Cats and kittens may be obtained free, but pedigree cats cost quite a lot depending on quality. With a healthy cat, veterinary fees should not be too high for the first year. You will have to pay for initial vaccinations and neutering and again for yearly boosters. Feeding and holiday boarding costs are other regular costs to be worked out.

Choosing a kitten

When selecting a kitten choose the 'bold' individual who comes to you. There is little to choose between a male and female. Avoid any with discharges from the eyes or nose. Forget any who cough or sneeze or where there is signs of diarrhoea soiling underneath the tail. Steer clear of a kitten which is noticeably smaller than its litter mates. *Remember a cat is for life and is not a toy to be dispensed with.* Don't get a cat unless you are prepared to be responsible for its welfare.

Short haired breeds

For the purposes of this book we have divided cats into three main groups — short haired, long haired and distinctive. Short haired varieties are subdivided into British Short Hairs and Foreign Short Hairs.

British Short Hairs

These cats have dense fur, rounded faces, round eyes and thickset bodies. They come in many colours and are usually described as Tabby (various), Selfcolour, Bicolour (two colours) and Tricolour (three colours).

Foreign Short Hairs

These varieties are more finely boned, long-tailed with chisel shaped heads and almond shaped eyes. Abyssinian, Siamese, Russian and Burmese are included in this group.

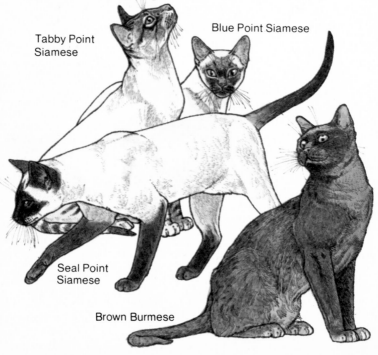

Tabby Point Siamese

Blue Point Siamese

Seal Point Siamese

Brown Burmese

Russian Blue

British Blue

Red Tabby

Cream

Brown Tabby

Tortoiseshell and White
(Tricolour)

Bicolour

7

Long haired breeds

Long haired cats are often regarded as the most attractive varieties and they require a lot of attention during grooming.

These Persian (Angora) cats come in many colours including Tabby, Selfcolour, Chinchilla (silver), Birman (golden beige), Colourpoint (cream or white body with darker markings on the points — ears, mask, legs, paws and tail), Bicolour (two colour), Tricolour (three colour), Cameo (mostly off-white) and Turkish (white with auburn markings).

Cream

Selfcoloured Red

Silver Tabby

Colourpoint

Birman

Tortoiseshell and White (Tricolour)

Chinchilla

Cameo

Bicolour (Magpie)

9

Distinctive cats

Though falling into the categories of the past four pages these cats are very obvious and usually rare. The Rex has a characteristic short smooth wavy coat, and the Manx (originating from Isle of Man, UK) is tailless.

The Lop-ear (Scottish fold eared) has definite droops to its ear-tips. The Balinese is often referred to as a long-haired Siamese and the Turkish Van cat is known as the swimming cat which has an affinity for water. The Oriental Spotted is supposed to be the nearest to the original cat known and revered in Ancient Egypt.

Korat

Havana

Cornish Rex

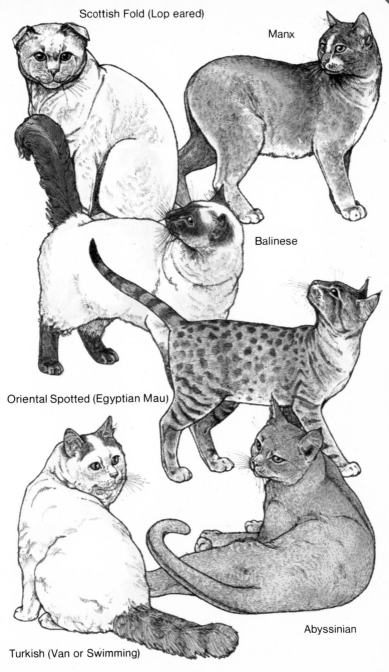

Scottish Fold (Lop eared)

Manx

Balinese

Oriental Spotted (Egyptian Mau)

Turkish (Van or Swimming)

Abyssinian

Travelling with your cat

Kittens and cats have to travel from their earliest days
— to their new homes, to the vet for vaccinations and
neutering operation, to be mated, and to their holiday
or boarding homes. You must therefore have a secure
transporting container made from either wicker,
plastic, or cardboard. Temporarily, a zip-up holdall
may be used *(provided it has air vents)*. For the trained
cat, a harness or collar may be secure enough.

Long journeys

Cats loose in a car are a positive danger to the driver
and in trains or coaches or aircraft they have to be
kept under stricter control. Where cats travel
separated from their owners, sedatives may be
prescribed by the vet though this should be avoided if
at all possible, for the cat's sake.

International travel poses additional problems
depending on the country you are entering.
Sometimes this will automatically mean compulsory
quarantine.

▼ **Plastic carrier which
converts easily into a bed.**

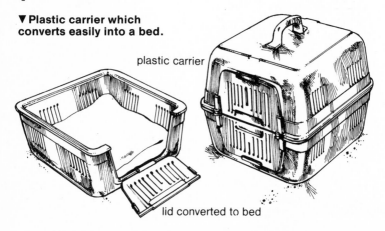

plastic carrier

lid converted to bed

No escapes
Cats must always travel securely - an escape is inexcusable. They are often happiest in the smallest possible space - curled up.

Ideally they should be able to see out but the more they see the more they yell. Such cats often travel better out of baskets. It is then essential to control them on harnesses and leads to prevent escape.

The cat is a bad subject for sedatives. Only after obtaining a vet's advice should these be used as a last resort. Get cats used to travelling especially if this is a regular part of your life.

holdall

carrying basket

cardboard carton

wire basket

Carrying your cat
There are many types of carriers and containers available from pet shops. Make sure that the one you buy is large enough for your cat.

A cardboard carton may be suitable to begin with but it soon wears and is not waterproof for very long. Basket carriers or those made from plastic or metal are more durable.

Holding and handling

This is the best way to pick up and hold a cat so that it feels secure. If it struggles you are unlikely to get scratched. Be careful not to press its neck too tightly.

As soon as kittens' eyes have opened it is necessary to handle them daily and frequently if they are not to become hand-shy and aggressive. There are right ways and wrong ways of doing this. An easily handled cat is essential in case it is necessary to give medicines or treat your pet. Correct handling will greatly lessen the risk of your getting scratched or bitten if the cat objects!

Remember that like you, a cat must be allowed to rest. It is only natural that it will object if you are too rough, if you disturb its sleep or if you handle it for too long a period. Always be firm but very gentle.

◄Gentle support
Mother cats will pick up and carry around very young kittens by holding the scruff of the neck. *This should never be done by you unless you support the body underneath.*

► Hold securely
Here is the best way of carrying a cat or kitten round the house. Usually the cat is relaxed and can be held securely against your body for longish periods. It is also the ideal way to pick it up or to place it in its basket.

If the cat struggles put it down on the ground gently and start again. Trying to hold a cat which is struggling will almost certainly result in a bit of scratching! A cat is as well-armed as a fighter!

◄Stroking your pet
Most cats resent lying on their backs - kittens less so. Take great care that if they attempt to roll upright they do not fall.

Cats like being stroked on the head, neck and down the back, but generally resent any undue handling.

15

Keeping a record

It is a good idea to keep a record of your kitten's activities from the first moment you take it home. You can choose from all sorts of exercise books, scrapbooks, photograph albums, ring binders, files or make your own cat-shaped book.

Keep medical cards handy
It's great fun to decorate the cover with your own 'cat' design. Label the cover carefully and keep it as a family album which everyone can enjoy reading. **Always** have the vet's name, telephone number, address and surgery hours handy. Keep a record of all visits to the vet and write down details of dates, vaccinations and medicines given to your kitten or cat.

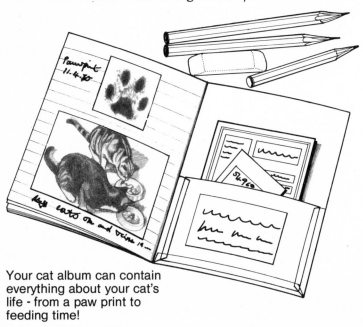

Your cat album can contain everything about your cat's life - from a paw print to feeding time!

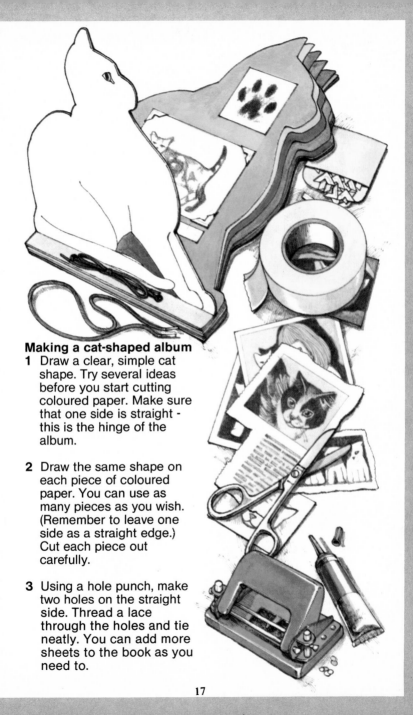

Making a cat-shaped album

1 Draw a clear, simple cat shape. Try several ideas before you start cutting coloured paper. Make sure that one side is straight - this is the hinge of the album.

2 Draw the same shape on each piece of coloured paper. You can use as many pieces as you wish. (Remember to leave one side as a straight edge.) Cut each piece out carefully.

3 Using a hole punch, make two holes on the straight side. Thread a lace through the holes and tie neatly. You can add more sheets to the book as you need to.

A bed for your kitten

It is not wise to let your cat sleep in your bed. Apart from being uncomfortable for you both there is always the chance that you may pick up fleas or some skin infection or germ from your pet. Cats are independent and like their own beds and should be made familiar with them from the very beginning.

The right place
Select a warm, draught-free spot where the bed will not be in anyone's way. The cat should have easy access to outside, its litter tray and food and water bowls during the night, so that it can help itself.

Kittens love getting into cardboard boxes and these make the best possible start before using a permanent bed.

Comfortable and warm

A wide range of cat beds are available — both covered and open. You can make them extra snug by lining the floor with newspaper, an old pillowcase and some sheepskin or a discarded woollie.

Don't make or buy one too large. If you watch sleeping cats they invariably curl up into a small shape and the tighter the fit, within reason, the better the cat likes its bed. A shoe-box will fit a tiny kitten and this can be changed as it grows.

A wide choice

For adult cats, a wicker or plastic bed is ideal. Choose one which is suitable for the place where it will be kept.

Ideally this will be where the cat can have access to it at all times, and where it will not be in the way.

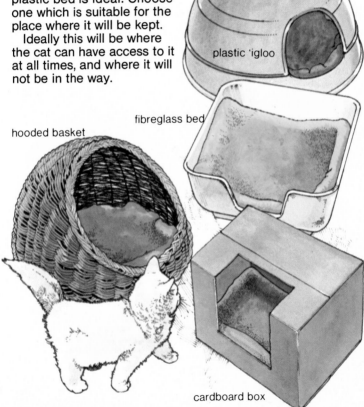

plastic 'igloo

fibreglass bed

hooded basket

cardboard box

Dirt boxes and cleanliness

1 hooded plastic litter box
2 plastic bowl
3 baking tray
4 soil
5 litter tray
6 scoops
7 manufactured litter
8 newspapers

Litter trays

Litter trays can be bought or made from a seed tray or
washing-up bowl. Special cat litter can be bought or
you can use peat, garden soil, wood shavings or
sawdust or even shredded newspaper. Cats are
naturally clean and require little if any training to use
a tray. As they get bigger they may prefer to use an
earth plot in the garden outside.

Cleaning the tray

Indwelling cats must always have a clean litter tray and a scoop can be used to assist with 'straining' soiled litter from clean. Litter can be burnt, or disposed of in the waste bin.

Naturally clean

All well cats are fastidiously clean and can be seen to wash themselves regularly, using their forelegs to reach inaccessible places. Their rough tongues are ideal for removing soiling from their coats. Cats also swallow large quantities of their own fur which they occasionally vomit as 'fur-balls'.

◄Kittens may only require a little tuition to start using their trays regularly.

A special system
Cats have a system of washing themselves starting with their back legs and tail. Then their forelegs and bib finishing with their midriff and lastly their faces.
  Unless ill, even a white cat keeps itself spotless, removing all traces of grime including fleas, loose hair and wetness from rain.

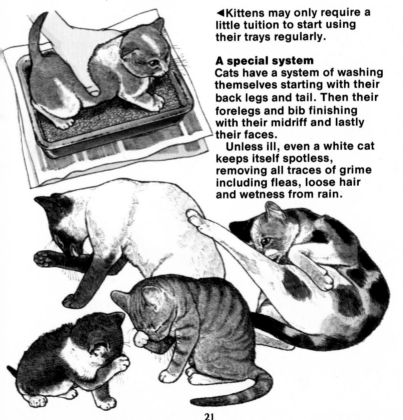

Feeding your cat

1 sprats
2 mackerel
3 liver
4 stewing meat
5 ground pet food
6 tinned food
7 dry food
8 semi-moist food

Cats enjoy and thrive on a wide range of fresh and manufactured pet foods. A small box of grass is often appreciated by flat-bound cats. They should have their own bowls for food, water and milk which should always be positioned in a quiet and easily washed area out of the way of people's feet. Cats prefer to be fed separately from the family and you should also wash their dishes separately.

1 earthenware
2 double plastic
3 plastic drinking bowl
4 metal dish
5 kitten dish
6 sealed grass box
7 grass growing

Collars, harnesses and name tags

Because of the curious position the cat has in the legal world, it is strongly advisable that all cats with access to outside have labels so that the owner can be notified in case of problems and accidents. If a cat wears a collar or harness, not only can an identity disc or tube be attached but also a bell to warn birds of approaching danger!

The right collar
Flea collars are not very good as identity collars and indeed may be harmful to cats, especially if they get wet in the rain, and they become less useful. When buying a collar or harness for a cat you should say that it is for a cat, because cat collars are made of elastic or have an insert of elastic so that when tree-climbing, a cat will not suffer if it ends up suspended by its collar. *Collars should not be too tight.* Replace the elastic if this becomes worn.

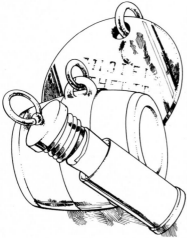

Identity tags
Identity tags come in the form of engraved discs, which are everlasting, or various tubes which contain 'messages' written on a paper insert.

Be sure to screw these up tightly to avoid loss and do not give the cat's name. Always offer a reward, but do not specify any set amount.

Remember your address
Give your full name and address (and remember to alter this if you move) and telephone number. Replace this insert message if you take your cat on holiday.

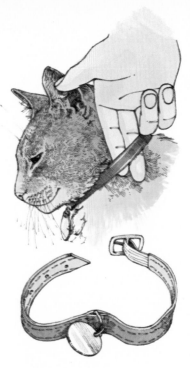

A good fit
A properly fitting collar should allow you to push two fingers through comfortably while the cat is wearing it. If the elastic is worn, it is easy to replace it on the whole collar.

Get your cat used to wearing a collar. It may try to scratch it off for a few minutes, but will soon accept it as part of its dress.

A cat harness
A harness is even better because it allows you to control your cat in a car or when visiting the vet etc. It should be adjustable so that as a kitten grows it will still provide a close fitting and secure control for your pet.

Flea collars
Flea collars are fabric or plastic material containing a chemical designed to kill fleas and other parasites.They are popular, but it is doubtful how useful they are. It is possible that they can cause eczema or even illness in some cats.

Grooming and bathing

Cats are largely self-grooming but all cats should be brushed daily if of the short haired varieties. If long haired, *it is absolutely essential* that they are not only brushed, but combed *at least* once daily to prevent the build-up of fur tangles which, if left, may eventually need veterinary attention. Grooming is a good excuse to trim claws occasionally if necessary.

Special grooming
Suitable combs and brushes (for use on the cat only), can be obtained from pet shops. It is also convenient to de-flea a cat during grooming using a suitable powder or aerosol. Don't do this daily, but at intervals recommended by your vet or as directed by instructions on the container. Cats (especially long hairs) can be also cleaned by dusting talc (French Chalk) into the hair and then brushing out thoroughly.

Some useful grooming aids are stiff brushes, combs (fine-tooth and coarse), nail cutters, and cat cosmetics like chalk powder and insecticidal (flea) preparations.

◀ Grooming long hairs
Long hairs require *daily* attention. Combing is essential to remove the dead undercoat especially on the tummy, between the front legs, behind the ears and the tail. If you don't do this, your cat may need an anaesthetic and a vet's knowledge to 'de-mat' it.

▶Grooming short hairs
Short hair cats require the minimum of grooming. Fine-tooth combing will remove loose fur and a strong brushing should follow. This is particularly important in old or sick cats. Breeders then use velvet or silk to give a final expert sheen to the coat.

▼Bathing
Bathing a cat should only be carried out in case of great flea infestation or heavy soiling. Most cats hate water so wet the cat gradually and work the shampoo in gently. Rinse very well. You may need someone to help you.

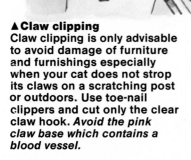

▲Claw clipping
Claw clipping is only advisable to avoid damage of furniture and furnishings especially when your cat does not strop its claws on a scratching post or outdoors. Use toe-nail clippers and cut only the clear claw hook. *Avoid the pink claw base which contains a blood vessel.*

Toys for your pet

Like children, kittens and cats enjoy playing and they learn at the same time. Soft toys and rolling toys like balls are particular favourites. Also paper twists, etc. suspended on thin elastic will be great fun. It is important not to play too roughly with your kitten because you could hurt it.

Kittens will retrieve small objects if they can be carried in the mouth. Be wary of string, cotton thread and elastic bands which cats love. These can be dangerous if they are swallowed. Place these objects safely out of reach in a drawer or cupboard.

You can make toys from ping-pong balls, screwed up tin foil, pipe cleaners shaped like a spider and cotton reels fitted with a bell at each end. Make quite sure that your kitten's toys are safe.

Making a toy fish

1 You will need felt, pins, needle, thread, scissors and a felt tip pen. Cut two fish shapes, one tail and two fins from brightly coloured felt.

▲ Cat mint
You can fill the fish with cat mint or 'catnip' because most cats really enjoy the smell of this herb. Dry quite a lot of leaves before you use them as stuffing in the toy you've made.

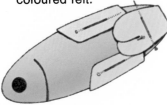

2 Pin the tail and both fins to the outside of one fish shape. Make the tail and fins jut over the edge at least ½ cm.

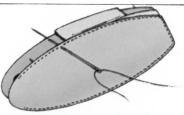

3 Place second fish shape - right side facing inwards - on top of piece pinned with tail and fins. Sew pieces together. Leave head open.

4 Stuff fish with dried cat mint through the opening you have left in the head.

Carefully stitch around the head. Draw in eyes and mouth with a pen.

Visiting the vet

Kittens rarely realize that their vet is their best friend! It is very valuable to let your vet check your cat or kitten as soon as possible after getting it. After a general check, your cat can be vaccinated to prevent it catching certain diseases, for example, cat flu, enteritis and in some countries, rabies.

Talking to the vet

These jabs are very important. The vet will be happy to answer your questions about breeding from a kitten, neutering, diet (what sort of food and how frequently) and any other points you may have. Apart from treating sick and injured animals, your vet, like your doctor, is anxious to prevent his patient becoming ill.

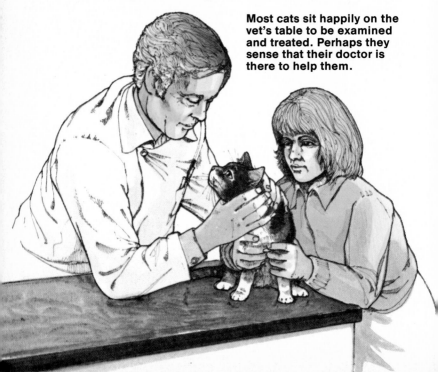

Most cats sit happily on the vet's table to be examined and treated. Perhaps they sense that their doctor is there to help them.

Your cat will probably require booster injections every year or so and you can ask the vet any further questions while going for regular check-ups. Injections do not hurt and rarely cause a cat to be even slightly unwell.

Early treatment
If your cat seems unwell and just wants to sleep and is off food, ask your vet to examine it as soon as possible. Early treatment can save suffering, expense and provides the best chance for speedy and complete recovery. Even the healthiest cat may have problems which need attention from time to time. The vet is your pet's best friend at these times.

Home treatment

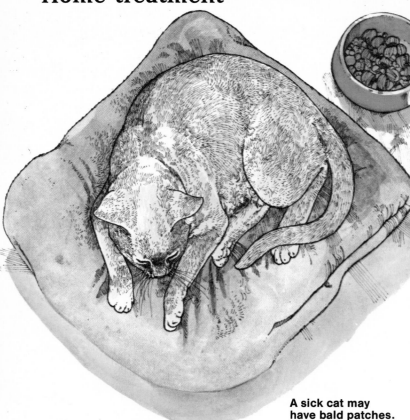

A sick cat may have bald patches.

Always look for abnormal behaviour in your cat — this is usually the first sign of illness and veterinary treatment may be needed. Look for signs of lack of appetite, extreme dullness and unwillingness to move. Undue vomiting or diarrhoea is abnormal, so is excessive thirst.

During grooming, any sign of skin sores or bald areas should not be ignored. Watery eyes and itchy ears, especially if there is excessive wax mean a trip to the vet. Coughing and sneezing can be signs of problems as can sudden weight loss.

Treating your cat

After examination the vet will often prescribe treatment for your cat and this may mean that you must instil ear or eye drops, give liquid medicine or tablets and carefully control the diet. Of course, always follow the instructions completely. It is not always possible to give drugs in food, for the cat may not wish to eat, especially if it suspects the food has been 'doctored'.

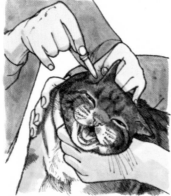

◄Ear and eye drops
Hold your cat steady - if you have trouble get assistance. Place the required number of drops down the widest passage of the ear, which is seen easily. After application do not allow the cat to shake its head until you have gently massaged the drops down. For eyes, hold the head steady. Allow the cat to blink.

►Giving liquids
Liquid should be given to a cat by holding the head steady (with assistance if necessary) and slightly upwards. Trickle fluid into mouth gently, ½ tea-spoonful at a time and allow the cat to swallow.

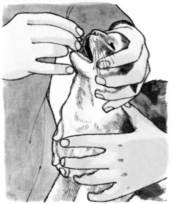

◄Tablets and capsules
Tablets and capsules are given by holding the cat securely and opening the mouth tilted upwards. The pill or tablet is dropped at the back of the throat and the cat is allowed to swallow this with mouth kept closed.

Parasites, inside and out

Where to look for parasites

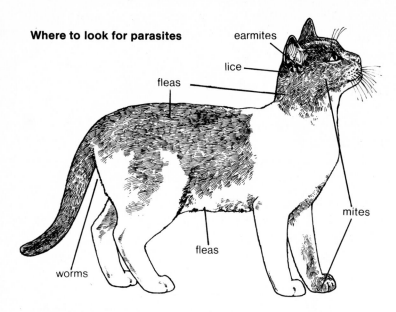

earmites

lice

fleas

mites

fleas

worms

The common internal parasites of cats include **tapeworms** (transmitted by swallowing fleas and eating mice, etc.) and **roundworms**. The tapeworms cause little trouble and few symptoms, but the roundworms should be dosed against in kittenhood and at regular intervals of roughly three months afterwards.

Drugs vary and you should ask your vet as to the best medicine and the correct dose. Worms can be recognised easily in the excreta.

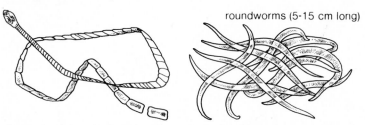

roundworms (5-15 cm long)

tapeworm (segments = grain of rice)

External parasites are common in the cat, particularly **fleas** which are often found in warm weather. Cats often become allergic to fleas which make them scratch and develop skin sores.

Treating parasites

Fortunately all external parasites are soon cleared up with lotions, aerosols, dusting powders or baths. The treatment may have to be repeated regularly.

Fleas can easily be seen round the neck and down the spine. **Lice** are found around the head. **Mites**, barely visible to the naked eye are detected by the damage they cause to the skin of the head or feet. You may also see a large amount of wax coming from affected ears. This depends on the mite which worries your cat. Treat external mites carefully because some can be transmitted to you.

flea

louse

tick

earmite

blowfly maggots

▲ Some cat pests
(not drawn to scale).

Accident!

Cats are more prone to accidents than other pets because they enjoy roaming freely and they are very inquisitive and playful. Cats are frequently injured as they cross roads when looking for mates. As they catch birds, flies and moths, many a cat takes a tumble from high windows or balconies.

When moving injured cats, keep them still to avoid increasing any damage by struggling. Keep them lying as flat as possible, e.g. on a tray, covered with a blanket, or confined securely in their carrying box.

Kittens enjoy wrestling with electric flex, so loop these up high out of reach and switch off wall plugs.

Cats tend to get under your feet especially at feeding times, so beware of tripping if carrying hot kettles or saucepans. If possible close the kitchen door.

Cleaning the fur
If a cat's paws or fur become covered with oil, or other chemicals, harmful effects may follow if it is allowed to lick itself clean and then swallows the poison.

If you see a cat covered in floor polish, bleach, or disinfectant *it is very important to cleanse the area well with soap (or detergent) and water.* This may mean bathing the cat.

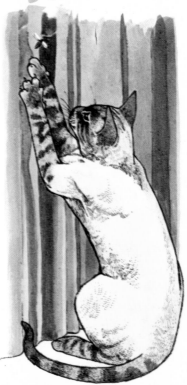

► **Stings**
In summer, cats will chase, catch and swallow flies, wasps, moths, etc. Usually this is quite harmless unless they get stung in the process!

A sting is rarely serious but a swelling may develop which is uncomfortable until it subsides in about 2 hours.

Make the cat comfortable by bathing the sting with lemon juice or rub with an onion.

Do not use fly-sprays or garden chemicals when your cat is around.

Making a cat door

A cat door (cat-flap) will allow a cat free access out to the garden for toilet and exercise and easy return indoors for warmth, dryness and protection. Many owners lock the door shut at night to prevent risk of accidents in the dark.

Keeping out intruders

Beware of other cats straying in to the house through the flap and attacking your cat or eating its food. Cats and kittens learn quickly how to use the door but a little bit of instruction may be needed at the beginning.

Cat doors are particularly useful where owners are out most of the day, allowing the cat in and out without the risk of burglaries which might result from leaving a window open. A good cat flap should be heavy enough to resist wind but still light enough for the cat to open.

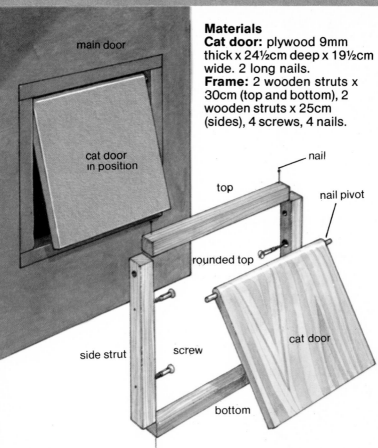

main door

cat door in position

Materials
Cat door: plywood 9mm thick x 24½cm deep x 19½cm wide. 2 long nails.
Frame: 2 wooden struts x 30cm (top and bottom), 2 wooden struts x 25cm (sides), 4 screws, 4 nails.

nail

top

nail pivot

rounded top

side strut

screw

cat door

bottom

What to do

1 With the help of an adult, make a hole (35cm deep x 30cm wide) in the main door, about 10cm from the bottom of the door.

2 Sand the top of the cat door, (19½cm wide) until the edge is rounded. About 1½cm from top, insert a nail on both sides leaving about 1cm jutting out. Saw off nail heads. Shafts of nails act as pivots for cat door.

3 Drill 3 holes in each side strut, 1½cm from top, 6cm from top and 6cm from bottom. Insert pivots into side struts. Nail top and bottom struts to side struts.

4 Screw assembled frame (plus cat door) into main door. Paint cat door and frame. Fit bolt to both doors to keep secure at night.

Smell and hearing

Cats — wild and domestic — have a very well developed sense of smell which is used in tracking prey of all sorts. It also allows the cat to sense danger approaching often long before it can be seen, and allows a cat to know good meat from bad and edible from inedible. For this reason cats rarely swallow poisons, even if they are hidden in tasty food.

Recognizing friends

Manufacturers make cat foods that attract the cat by smell and flavour. Smell is closely linked with taste and cats can often be seen sniffing their gardens, owners and homes to find out if a stranger or stray cat has been around. The acute sense of smell allows cats not only to identify other cats but to know whether they are friends or enemies and what mood they are in.

Hearing is probably the cat's best developed sense. The inside of the ear not only contains the intricate organ of hearing but also very sensitive balancing equipment. The ear flaps are relatively large, which enables the cat to catch all sound waves, even faint ones.

Early warning system
Hearing in the cat is important as a safety measure to give early warning of attack, to detect food or prey and as a means of communication. The position of the ear flaps often tells you what mood your cat is in. If it's alert and interested, the ears are pricked upright and forward and twitch to catch every sound. If it's annoyed or very aggressive the ears are held backwards and very flat to the head.

Hunting — tongue and teeth

The tongue of the cat is quite unusual. The top surface is covered by many horny spikes which give a rough texture. This helps cats to drink by curling the tongue to trap the water or milk on the rough surface. When eating solid food, the rough surface helps to grip the food and places it at the back of the throat where it is gulped down.

Grooming aid

The roughness is so developed in wild cats that the tongue is used in preference to the teeth to rip off large chunks of meat from prey. The tongue is long and very mobile and this helps with self-grooming, but the surface is inclined to trap many loose hairs which are then swallowed. Another function of the tongue is taste which is very well developed in the cat.

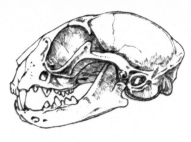 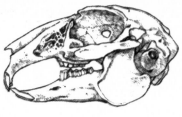

A cat's skull showing the front teeth (incisors), the large sharply pointed fangs (canines), next to the canines are pre-molars then molars.

Because it is herbivore (vegetarian) the rabbit has fewer front teeth. There are more rear teeth (molars) for chewing and grinding food.

Meat eaters

Cats are basically carnivores (meat-eaters) and their teeth are therefore adapted to slicing, biting and tearing rather than grinding. The prominent eye-teeth or fangs (canines) were originally used for catching and killing food in the wild and then for tearing the flesh. The adult teeth don't appear until about 6 months of age or so.

Younger kittens have milk teeth which show shortly after birth and are pushed out by the permanent teeth. If you look carefully at a cat's mouth you will find the upper and lower teeth only just overlap like a pair of scissors. Unlike ours, a cat's jaw can hardly move sideways.

Cats' eyes

Cats are nocturnal animals — which means they are night hunters. They have very large eyes with an ability to alter the shape of the pupil. In bright light their vision is poor but because of their sense of smell and hearing this is not so important.

Each eye is protected by three lids and the eyeballs can rotate freely in their sockets to follow movements, much more than in other animals. Kittens are born blind and their eyelids open at 7 – 10 days. At night, if a bright light shines into their eyes it is reflected from a green layer at the back. This fact was noticed and adapted to make the road markings which are called 'cats' eyes'.

►Bright light

In bright light the pupil (black part) of the eye is narrowed down to a vertical slit. This reduces the amount of light entering the eye, and also the field of vision. As the light becomes dimmer the pupil widens gradually to allow more light to enter. This improves vision greatly.

►Dark conditions

In very dark conditions the pupil will be fully open and is quite round. The coloured part of the eye (the iris) is just a narrow strip surrounding the pupil and this is when you can see clearly the green reflecting layer at the back of the eye (retina) which is called the tapetum.

►Third eyelid

The front of the eye is protected by an upper and lower lid and a third 'haw' (nictitating membrane) which shows distinctly when cats are unwell. The main function of this seems to be cleansing of the clear front layer of the eye (the cornea), like windscreen wipers in a car.

►Odd-eyed cats

Some cats are bred with odd coloured eyes. The most common is the odd-eyed White short hair which has one blue and one orange eye. They are sometimes deaf, which is linked with blue eye colour, (but this is not always so).

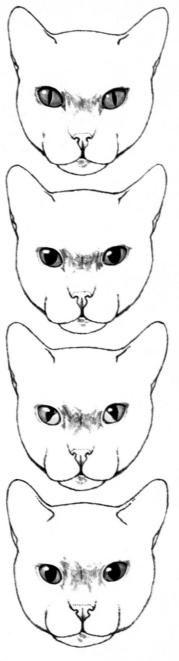

Perfect balance

Cats have an uncanny sense of balance. They are nature's acrobats and with the help of a mobile tail as a counterweight, and very strong sharp hooklike claws, they find climbing no effort at all. They rarely fall and they can perch and walk on very narrow structures like tightrope walkers in a circus.

Their remarkable balance also enables them to right themselves if they fall, so that they invariably land feet first. Many people believe that this is the origin of the saying 'nine lives' of cats because they often avoid serious injury when falling.

retracted claws   extended claws   front paw   back paw

Claws on all four feet can be unsheathed to attack or to grip something.

The five hooked front claws are often unsheathed. Back claws are used for leaping.

▼ Falling

The great agility of cats is seen from earliest age when falling. Using the sensitive balancing mechanism in the inner ear the cat senses its problem and rolls, front half first so that forelegs and then back legs are downwards and will hit the ground first.

This cushions the body and prevents serious injury.

▲ Climbing

Cats can climb up and down vertical heights which are many hundreds of metres high. Their formidable claws give great grip and their fine balancing gives their head for heights.

Most cats descend from high trees tail first and when within reach of the ground twist round and leap to land feet first.

The many moods of a cat

As you watch your cat you will find it has all sorts of
moods which you will easily recognize. These include
aggression, contentment, pleasure and noseyness.
Even pet domestic cats go through the actions of
stalking, hunting and killing prey as if living in the wild
— right from kittenhood. Most cats will catch flies,
birds etc. not because they are cruel but in play.

Understanding your cat
The moods shown by the cat will give an idea of what
you can expect. For example, an angry or frightened
cat should not be picked up, in case it attacks and
injures you. On the other hand a relaxed, friendly and
purring cat can be handled and stroked, usually with
complete safety.

▶ A contented cat
A purring cat may still wag its tail and may stretch in sheer contentment. This is a sign of complete relaxation and indicates that the cat can be petted and handled safely.

◀ Showing pleasure
Cats also show pleasure by rubbing themselves against your legs, especially after fussing or feeding or when they expect food. It is thought that by doing this, certain glands are stimulated and a particular scent is left on objects they've rubbed against which can be smelt by other cats.

▶ A cross cat
A cat showing signs of annoyance will cease purring and the tail tip will twitch. Eventually the whole tail will wag furiously as the cat becomes more upset. Such annoyance may be shown towards a fly near at hand.

◀ Showing anger
A very angry or frightened cat is dangerous and can easily be spotted by the fluffed-up fur particularly on the tail ('Bottle-brush'). The back is usually arched and the cat stands side-on to the 'enemy'. The lips are drawn back in a snarl and the cat is very noisy. It will spit and growl. Beware of such an animal!

How to make a scratching post

You will find that cats love to scratch, tear and rip furniture and carpets unless you make or buy a scratching post which they can use instead. A cat scratches to remove the outer shells of its front claws. During this scratching, cats also exercise and stretch their whole bodies.

A young kitten will need to be trained to use a scratching post. Hold its paw and scratch the post gently. This way it will learn to use the post — not your furniture!

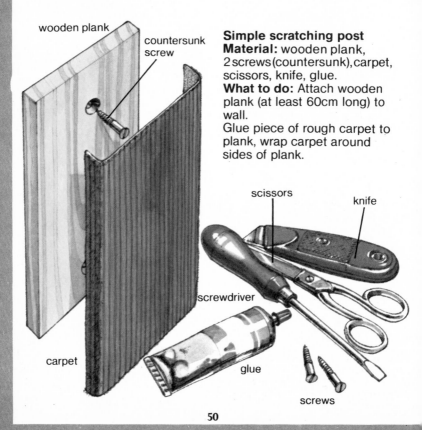

Simple scratching post
Material: wooden plank, 2 screws (countersunk), carpet, scissors, knife, glue.
What to do: Attach wooden plank (at least 60cm long) to wall.
Glue piece of rough carpet to plank, wrap carpet around sides of plank.

wooden plank

countersunk screw

scissors

knife

screwdriver

carpet

glue

screws

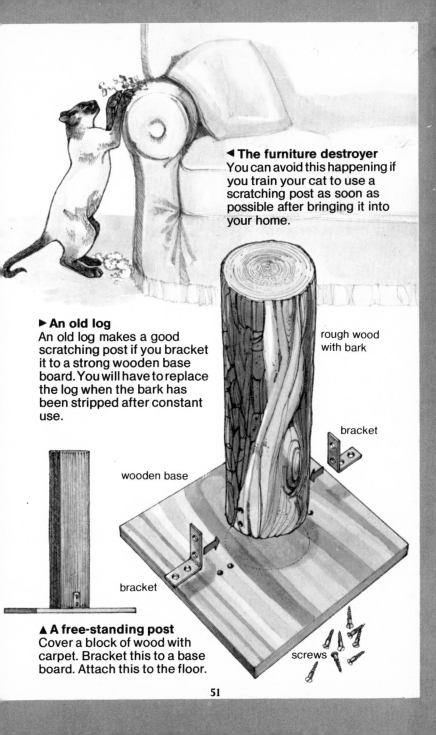

◄ The furniture destroyer
You can avoid this happening if you train your cat to use a scratching post as soon as possible after bringing it into your home.

► An old log
An old log makes a good scratching post if you bracket it to a strong wooden base board. You will have to replace the log when the bark has been stripped after constant use.

rough wood with bark

bracket

wooden base

bracket

▲ A free-standing post
Cover a block of wood with carpet. Bracket this to a base board. Attach this to the floor.

screws

Holiday care

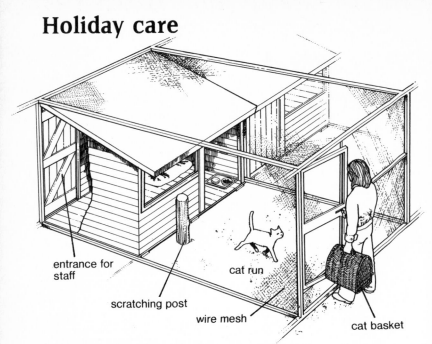

entrance for staff

cat run

scratching post

wire mesh

cat basket

▲ **An owner collecting a cat from the cattery**

Book early

The law requires that you make provision for your cat when you go on holiday, so you should book it into a good cattery in advance.

It is a good plan to inspect catteries before the time arrives to see that they do live up to their advertisements. Remember, that like hotels, they have their busy seasons and there are many fewer catteries than hotels.

Leaving your cat at home

If your cat is staying at home you must arrange for a reliable relation or neighbour to feed and care for it while you're away. Remember to leave plenty of usual foods and full instructions for the person acting as caretaker.

Too many cats

There are hundreds of unwanted cats born every year. As diseased strays, they have to hunt for food where they can find it.

Birth control

Far too many kittens are born every year and it is a simple and permanent job for a vet to neuter your kitten (of either sex) from about five months of age. This stops the production of yet more unwanted kittens. The operation usually means a kitten staying about a day at the vet's hospital. Another visit may be necessary in about one week for stitch removal in the case of a female.

Kittens make a very quick recovery from the operation and there are normally no side effects. Cats of any age can be neutered, so if you acquire an adult, it can also be neutered easily.

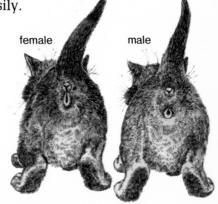

female   male

Male or female?
Sexing cats can be difficult - this picture will help. The easy way to tell is the space between the two rear openings, which is greater in the male.

Nearly all tortoiseshell cats will be female but not all ginger cats are toms (males).

When your cat has kittens

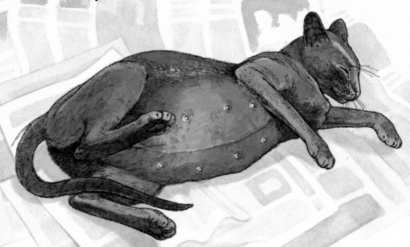

Unneutered female cats allowed access to a tomcat will probably produce kittens. Kittens take roughly nine weeks to develop from mating till birth. Usually the first signs of pregnancy is the fattening of the mother cat and later the development of the breasts which produce milk. The mother finally prepares a comfortable bed for giving birth.

When the birth is near, extra food and vitamins may be required. A quiet, clean area should be chosen for the 'nesting box' where the birth and early suckling can go on without interruptions. Kittens should not be handled until their eyes are open.

A kitten is born blind and its eyes do not usually open until it is 7 - 10 days old. The claws remain extended until the kitten is about 4 weeks old.

Historical cats

Cats have played an important part in people's lives for thousands of years.

They have been worshipped in some countries and sacrificed in others. They are believed to bring good luck and bad luck.

Here are a few strange cats and cat sayings. Perhaps you can collect some more?

1. The Cheshire Cat. An imaginary cat who appears in *'Alice in Wonderland'*, a children's story by Lewis Carroll.

2. The witch's black cat. Black cats were thought to be devils who helped witches to bring bad fortune.

3. 'It's raining cats and dogs' is an old saying which refers to very heavy rainfall.

4. An Egyptian cat mummy. Cats were often given formal burial and then mummified.

5. Black cats and horseshoes are thought to bring good luck in some countries.

6. The Egyptian goddess Pasht. She was often shown as a cat or with a cat's head.

7. 'Nine lives of a cat'. This saying refers to a cat's amazing ability to fall without injuring itself.

8. Cat o'nine tails. This was a rope whip with nine knotted lashes often used as a punishment on board ship.

Reference section

Useful Addresses

There are many good sources of information about cats and listed below are a number of contact addresses which should provide a lot of information you may need. **The Governing Council of the Cat Fancy** (GCCF) is to the cat world in U.K. what the Kennel Club is to Dogs. It is GCCF who register breeding cats and their offspring, and they also approve cat clubs and shows. Most enquiries can therefore be addressed to:-

The Governing Council of the Cat Fancy,
Doverfields,
Petworth Road,
Witley,
Surrey.

Feline Advisory Bureau is a charity whose aim is to protect the well-being of the cat both physical and emotional. This organisation advises owners of cats on all aspects of management, illness, disease and welfare. It is advisable to become a member of FAB to receive quarterly bulletins, free advice, and inexpensive publications covering most aspects of cat welfare.

Write to:-
FAB,
6 Woodthorpe Road,
Putney,
London SW15.

Vets and Animal Welfare Groups
The vet closest to your home is usually the best person with whom to register your cat as a patient. Consult Yellow Pages Telephone Directory or ask an animal-owning neighbour to recommend one. Lists of local practices are also kept at the library and at police stations. If still in difficulty contact the following for lists:-
British Veterinary Association,
7 Mansfield Street,
London W1M 0AT

The Pet Health Council,
4th Floor, Walter House,
418-422 Strand,
London WC2R 0PL

Pedigree Petfoods Education Centre can supply advice especially on school cat projects. They can be contacted at:-
Stanhope House,
Stanhope Place,
London W2 2HH

Welfare Societies

There are many charities involved with cats. Here are a few you can contact in case of difficulty:-

People's Dispensary for Sick Animals,
P.D.S.A. House,
South Street,
Dorking,
Surrey, RG4 2LB

Royal Society for the Prevention of Cruelty to Animals,
The Manor House,
Horsham,
Sussex.

Universities Federation for Animal Welfare,
8 Hamilton Close,
South Mimms,
Potters Bar,
Herts EN6 3QD.

Cats Protection League,
20 North Street,
Horsham,
Sussex.

For help in dealing with wild or stray cats contact:-
Cat Action Trust,
The Crippetts,
Deanwood Road,
Jordans,
Beaconsfield,
Bucks.

Cats in Industry,
154 Tom Lane,
Sheffield 10.

Boarding Catteries
These can be found by searching Yellow Pages, or by asking at the local vet or RSPCA. Lists of inspected and approved catteries are available from Feline Advisory Bureau and Cats Protection League (addresses on P.58 and P.59).

Advance booking
Remember that it is illegal to abandon a cat when you go on holiday and absolutely cruel to make inadequate arrangements for this period for your cat to be cared for properly. Also remember that like hotels, catteries get fully booked, so plan well ahead.

Emergency help
Important - never make a 'blind' booking for your cat's holidays. Always visit the cattery before confirming arrangements to satisfy yourself that the housing and care is of a good standard.

A scheme for emergency boarding - e.g. where a single owner is suddenly taken to hospital - is operated by:—
Animal Welfare Trust,
47 Whitehall,
London SW1.

Cat Shows

These are a very good source of cat books of all kinds. You can also buy accessories such as collars and leads, litter trays, beds, cat-flaps and toys of all descriptions. Shows also give you a chance of meeting breeders of your favourite cats and discussing any problems or questions you may have with them. You can also see, compare, and judge your cat against the rest, speak to the judges and determine where your cat has its failings.

Cat Clubs

These are mushrooming all over the country, and if you are keen you must become a member. Clubs' information is obtainable from GCCF. They may be grouped geographically e.g. South West Counties Cat Club, or by breed - e.g. Havana and Foreign Lilac Cat Club. There really are clubs and groups to suit all tastes whether you own a 'moggy' or any type of thoroughbred cat. It is through these organisations that you can, as a keen cat fancier, progress with a show and breeding career because of your dedication to your favourite breed of cat.

Cat Equipment

Generally most cat shows have stalls selling all accessories for cats mentioned in this book. Also pet shops stock a comprehensive range of feeding bowls, litter trays, cat beds, toys, collars and tack, and brushes, as do many larger department stores with pet sections. However listed below are some suppliers specialising in 'cat-ware':-

Cats Accessories, Ltd.,
Catac House,
1 Newnham Street,
Bedford MK40 3JR

Uropets,
7 Northcote Road,
London NW10 9LL

E & J Accessories,
237 Fore Street,
Edmonton,
London N18

Ladymead Pet Supplies Ltd.,
5 Trinity Road,
Luton,
Beds.

Catty Goods
Catz,
25 Bedfordbury,
London WC2N 4BL

Pet Health Insurance,
Pet Plan Ltd.,
Freepost,
32 Wood Lane,
London W12.

Booklist

For light, entertaining reading, information and reference, the list of books for cat enthusiasts is endless. Most titles can be obtained from your local library or bookshop.

Cats & Catdom Annual (from the same publishers as Fur & Feather)
Watmoughs Ltd.,
Idle,
Bradford,
W. Yorkshire BD108 NL.

Cats & Cat Care by Henderson & Coffey (David & Charles)

Cats in the Belfry by Dorothy Foster (Harrap)

A Dictionary of Cat Lovers by Christabel Aberconway (Michael Joseph)

The World of Cats by John Montgomery (Hamlyn)

The Colourful World of Cats (Marks & Spencer)

Jones Animal Nursing (BSAVA, Pergamon Press)

Heath's Aid to Nursing Small Animals (BSAVA Bailliere Tindall)

Cats, their health and care (Farming Press Ltd)

Introducing cats as pets (Hamlyn)

Champion Cats of the World by Catherine Ing and Grace Pond (Harrap)

Cats by Christine Metcalf (Hamlyn)

Understanding Cats by Bridget Gibbs (Usborne)

Guide to Cats of the World by Howard Loxton (Elsevier Phaidon)

Observer's Book of Cats by Grace Pond (Warne)

The Intelligent Cat by Grace Pond and Angela Sayer (Davis-Poynter)

Understanding Your Cat by Michael Fox (Blond and Briggs)

Bookshops
Jean Pratt,
The Little Bookshop,
Farnham Common,
Bucks.

Cat Medical Books
Bailliere Tindall,
35 Red Lion Square,
London WC1R 4SG.

Kimptons Medical Bookshop,
205 Great Portland Street,
London W1

Glossary

Booster: vaccination given to older cats to increase protection against disease.

Bottle-brush tail: fluffed up tail fur usually showing aggression.

Breed: cats of the same type.

Cattery: establishment where cats are bred or boarded.

Cat flap: flap fitted usually in door to allow free access in and out of house.

Cat flu: an illness affecting cats, resembling a human cold.

Cross-bred: cat from parents of different breeds.

Debutante: cats that have never been exhibited before.

Dew claws: nails equivalent to human thumbs, found on front paws.

Ear mites: parasites cuasing irritation in cats' ears.

Enteritis: a serious disease of cats which can cause severe vomiting and diarrhoea.

Entire: un-neutered cat.

Flea collars: plastic or fabric collars impregnated with a chemical to kill fleas.

Fleas: insects which commonly live in cats' fur.

Fur balls: collection of fur in cat's stomach swallowed while grooming.

Grooming: general care of a cat, including brushing and combing.

Haws: third eyelids or nictitating membranes.

Junior: cat under 2 years old.

Litter: materials used in toilet trays.

Neuter: cat prevented from breeding by surgical operation.

Neutering: operation variously called speying, spaying, fixing, doctoring, castration, dressing.

Non-pedigree (mongrel): cat of no special breed.

Novice: cats that have not won a first prize.

Pedigree (pure-bred): cat bred from ancestors of a specific breed. Also the document showing ancestry.

Queen: female cat.

Scratching post: an upright pillar on which kittens can be trained to strop their claws.

Senior: cats 2 years of age or older.

Tom: male cat.

Vaccination (inoculation): protection against specific diseases, usually given by injection.

Veteran: cats over 6 years.

Weaning: the time of change-over for kittens from suckling mother to solid food.

Index